HOORAY FOR CHEFS!

by Kurt Waldendorf

BUMBA BOOKS™

LERNER PUBLICATIONS ◆ MINNEAPOLIS

Note to Educators:

Throughout this book, you'll find critical thinking questions. These can be used to engage young readers in thinking critically about the topic and in using the text and photos to do so.

Lerner Publications Company
A division of Lerner Publishing Group, Inc.
241 First Avenue North
Minneapolis, MN 55401 USA

For reading levels and more information, look up this title at www.lernerbooks.com.

Library of Congress Cataloging-in-Publication Data

Names: Waldendorf, Kurt, author.
Title: Hooray for chefs! / by Kurt Waldendorf.
Other titles: Hooray for community helpers!
Description: Minneapolis : Lerner Publications, [2017] | Series: Bumba books—Hooray for community helpers! | Audience: Ages 4–8. | Audience: K to grade 3. | Includes bibliographical references and index.
Identifiers: LCCN 2016001265 (print) | LCCN 2016008838 (ebook) | ISBN 9781512414394 (lb : alk. paper) | ISBN 9781512414691 (pb : alk. paper) | ISBN 9781512414707 (eb pdf)
Subjects: LCSH: Cooks—Juvenile literature.
Classification: LCC TX652.5 .W3325 2017 (print) | LCC TX652.5 (ebook) | DDC 641.5092—dc23

LC record available at http://lccn.loc.gov/2016001265

Manufactured in the United States of America
1 – VP – 7/15/16

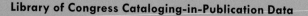

LERNER
SOURCE

Expand learning beyond the printed book. Download free, complementary educational resources for this book from our website, www.lernerresource.com.

Table of Contents

Meal Makers

Chefs make food for people

to eat.

Chefs work in kitchens.

Chefs know what tastes good.

They put foods together.

They use recipes.

Chefs prepare ingredients.

They cut and chop.

Why do you think some ingredients need to be cut?

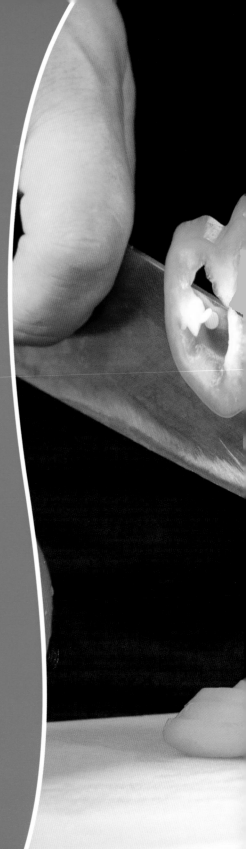

Chefs mix the ingredients.

They cook them.

This chef fries vegetables in a pan.

Pastry chefs bake.

They make desserts.

This chef bakes muffins and rolls.

Can you think of other foods a pastry chef bakes?

Chefs choose foods for menus.

People choose food from

the menus.

Some people go to school to become chefs.

Other people learn in kitchens.

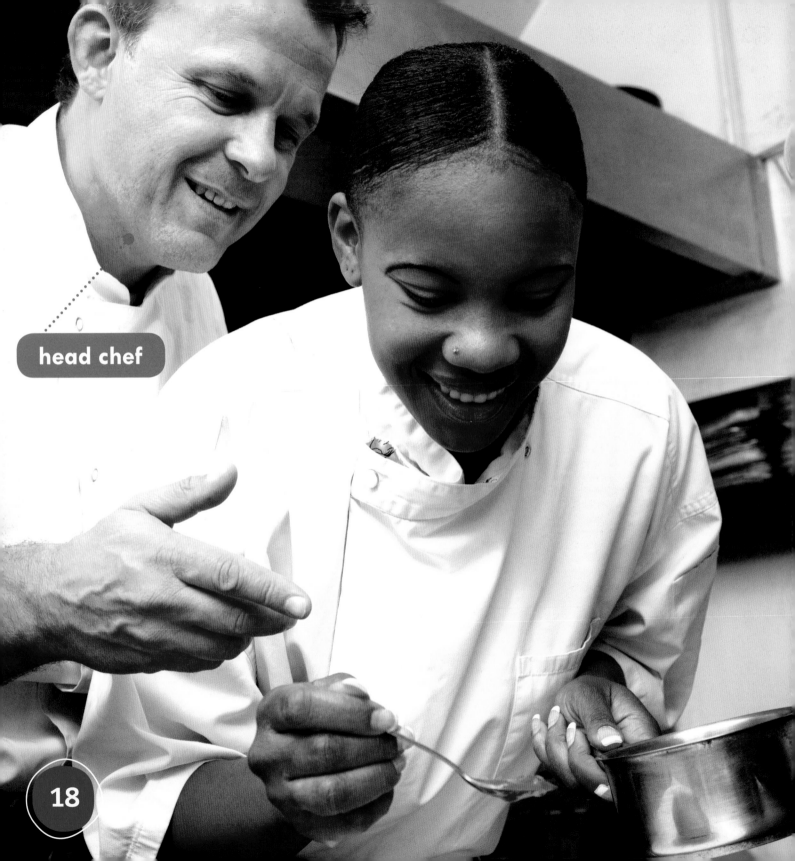

head chef

Chefs work hard to be head chefs.

Head chefs are in charge

of kitchens.

Why do you think kitchens need head chefs?

Chefs work in many places with kitchens. They help people enjoy food.

Chef Tools

pots and pans

oven

oven mitts

baking pan

stove

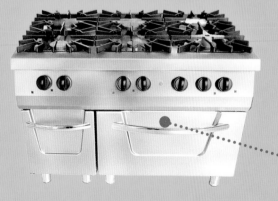

knife

Picture Glossary

ingredients

food used to make a recipe

menus

lists of food choices at a restaurant

pastry chefs

chefs who make sweet baked goods

recipes

instructions for making food

23

Index

Read More

Askew, Amanda. *Chef.* Irvine, CA: QEB, 2010.

Liebman, Dan. *I Want to Be a Chef.* Buffalo, NY: Firefly Books, 2012.

Neister, Kari. *Chefs.* Minneapolis: Bullfrog Books, 2015.

Photo Credits

The images in this book are used with the permission of: © Nick White/DigitalVision/Thinkstock, p. 5; © michaeljung/Shutterstock.com, p. 6; © Zorandim/Shutterstock.com, pp. 8–9; © Oktay Ortakcioglu/iStock.com, p. 10; © otnaydur/Shutterstock.com, pp. 13, 23 (bottom left); © Intellistudies/Shutterstock.com, pp. 14, 23 (top right); © wavebreakmedia/Shutterstock.com, p. 17; © Monkey Business Images/Shutterstock.com, p. 18; © goodluz/Shutterstock.com, pp. 20–21; © sevenke/Shutterstock.com, p. 22 (top left); © Mon's Images/Shutterstock.com, p. 22 (top middle); © Vereshchagin Dmitry/Shutterstock.com, pp. 22 (top right), 22 (bottom left); © cretolamna/Shutterstock.com, p. 22 (middle left); © Robyn Mackenzie/Shutterstock.com, p. 22 (bottom right); © Matt Antonino/Shutterstock.com, p. 23 (top left); © Fertnig/iStock.com, p. 23 (bottom right).

Front Cover: © sheff/Shutterstock.com.